DON'T DIE WITHOUT ME

Take care of your family with this step-by-step guide to planning your funeral and final wishes

🐢 Turtle Publishing

Copyright © 2022 by Claire Hoffman & Rose Gilder
All rights reserved.

No part of this publication may be reproduced, distributed, or transmitted in any form by any means, including photocopying, recording, or other electronic methods without the prior written permission of the authors, except in the case of brief quotations embodied in reviews and certain other noncommercial uses permitted by copyright law. For permission requests, please contact the authors.

First printed in 2022.
Printed on demand in United States, Australia and United Kingdom.

Cover & Interior Design Kathy Shanks from Turtle Publishing

Published by Turtle Publishing

Well of Grief
© David Whyte

Those who will not slip beneath
the still surface of the well of grief,

turning downward through its black water
to the place we cannot breathe,

will never know the source from which we drink,
the secret water, cold and clear,

nor find in the darkness, glimmering,

the small round coins,
thrown by those who wished for something else.

TABLE OF CONTENTS

FROM THE AUTHOR vii

PART I
Setting the Scene

PLANNING FOR THE UNEXPECTED 3
WHAT DOES IT MEAN TO DIE IN AUSTRALIA? 3
   LEGAL DOCUMENTS 4
   MY PRIORITIES FOR END-OF-LIFE CARE 7
   POST-DEATH DESIRES 7

PART II
My Death

STEP 1
Decide how I want to die — 11

VALUES AND SPIRITUAL PREFERENCES 12
PREFERENCES ON PLACES TO DIE 14
LIFE-SUSTAINING TREATMENTS 16
   DO NOT RESUSCITATE (DNR) 28

STEP 2
Decide who will speak on my behalf — 31

MEDICAL TREATMENT DECISIONS 32
QUALITIES OF MY DECISION MAKER 32
SPEAKING TO MY GP 33
PUTTING IT ON PAPER 34

STEP 3
Decide who I need to tell and who family should contact — 35

- MY FAMILY — 35
- MY SOCIAL SUPPORT NETWORK — 37
- HEALTH, FINANCIAL & INSURANCE INSTITUTIONS — 38
- PUTTING IT ON PAPER: COMPLETE MY COMMUNICATION & CONNECTION PLAN — 39

STEP 4
What happens after I die? — 45

- CHOICES FOR MY BODY — 45
- DEATH NOTICES — 50
- PEOPLE TO TELL — 50
- PEOPLE, PETS AND POSSESSIONS — 51
- LOVE LETTERS — 52
- PUTTING IT ON PAPER — 53
- REVISIT, REFLECT & REVIEW — 53

PART III
My Life

- PEACE — 57
- WHAT IS MY LEGACY? — 59
- LIFE REVIEW — 60
- CHECKLIST OF NECESSARY ITEMS — 60

FROM THE AUTHORS

In May 2018 Claire's husband Garryn died. He was 42. The hours and days that followed were filled with a mixture of complete clarity and utter fog. It was hideous. The person she needed to plan this with wasn't there any longer.

They were young and had a 10-year-old daughter. They both thought they had time. Time to heal their wounds, time to work on their relationship. Time to get their finances sorted.

They didn't.

One lesson we have learnt from this experience is that time is not a guarantee. The unexpected happens every day and people are constantly encountering hardship and sorrow. We cannot always control when and where we are going to die, but there are things that we can control if the unexpected happens. We should plan for the unexpected and approach each day with a level of awareness that includes how little in control we actually are.

Garryn died and left his family with a mess to clean up and no way of helping Claire raise their daughter in the years to come. This book is designed to help you avoid this scenario.

Our hope is to generate a level of consciousness around our inevitable death in order to lessen the fear and allow a greater engagement in life.

Death can be messy.

Undertaking this process will enable you to feel at peace. A peace from knowing that if the unexpected does happen, your loved ones will have something to guide them – and in a way, although you will be gone, they will feel as though you are still with them while they work through what is to follow.

A difficult time will be less complicated.

This book is organized as a simple how-to guide with step-by-step instructions. Thinking and talking about death can be overwhelming, so the easier we can make it for you to navigate the process, the better.

The 'Don't' Die Without Me' Framework on the following page will help guide you through this book.

Claire & Rose

PART I — Setting the Scene

- Planning for the unexpected
- What does it mean to die in Australia?

PART II — My Death

WHAT ARE THE STEPS?	WHAT SHOULD I THINK ABOUT?	WHAT OUTCOME DO I NEED?
STEP 1 — Decide how I want to die	• Values & spiritual preferences • Preferences on places to die • Life sustaining treatments	Advanced Care Directive Document
STEP 2 — Decide who will speak on my behalf	• Medical treatment decisions • Qualities of my decision maker • Speaking to your GP	Appointment of Medical Treatment Decision Maker Document
STEP 3 — Decide who I need to tell/talk to	• My family • Social support network • Financial, health and insurance institutions	Communication & Connection Plan
STEP 4 — What happens after I die?	• Choices for my body • Choices for my heart • People, pets and possessions	Will, Funeral Plan & Letters of Love

REVISIT, REFLECT AND REVIEW

PART III — My Life

- Peace
- Legacy
- Life review

PART I

Setting the Scene

*Plan for what is great while it is easy;
Do what is great while it is small.*

Lao Tze

PLANNING FOR THE UNEXPECTED

Whether you are young or old, ill or in good health, giving death a seat at your table is necessary. Why? If we can embrace the fact that we are going to die, our lives become a whole lot more meaningful. We receive each moment with gratitude, and by embracing our own ultimate death, we also embrace the fact that all those we love will die. As a consequence of this acceptance, we treat others with tender love and kindness, as if it's the last time we will see them.

Imagine a world in which the majority acted with this level of awareness.

We also treat ourselves with more tender love and care, not sweating the small stuff as much, and instead think about how we want to live out this great gift of life we've been given. You cannot prevent death, but you may be able to direct how you want your final days to play out. Planning for the unexpected, or even the expected, ensures you get the care you want and avoid the things you don't want, even if you are unable to speak for yourself.

WHAT DOES IT MEAN TO DIE IN AUSTRALIA?

If you haven't taken responsibility for your ultimate death, dying in Australia can leave your family with quite an expensive burden. But the fact that you're reading this book shows that you're interested in doing what it takes to ensure that your loved ones are not left with a mess after your death. Below is listed the **necessary must haves** – regardless of your age. The fact is, if you've reached adulthood, you need these. You can always revisit them as the inevitable wheels of change carry you forward in life.

- Legal documents – Will, Power of Attorney, Advance Health Care Directive, Appointment of Substitute Medical Treatment Decision Maker;
- Practicalities with respect to your legal documents;
- Your priorities for end-of-life care;
- Common medical end-of-life interventions for you to ponder;
- Post-death desires.

LEGAL DOCUMENTS

Will

The time is **now** to get your legal documents in order, because if you go outside and get hit by a bus today, your family might find that you being hit by a bus wasn't the only bad thing to happen to them. If you die without a Will, you are considered as having died 'in intestacy', meaning you have not validly disposed of some or all of your assets, and as a result they will be distributed according to a legal formula. This could mean that your assets do not end up with the person/s you would have chosen, and also means you have no control over who distributes your assets. The rule of thumb is that your family will always be better off if you have a Will. Don't delay; it doesn't take long and will make you feel a lot more at ease.

If you do have a Will, is it up to date and easy to locate? If you don't have a Will, take care of this now.

Power of Attorney

Powers of Attorney (POAs) can be both general and enduring and allow you to appoint someone you trust to make decisions for you during your lifetime. These decisions may include:

Personal (including health) matters, which relate to personal or lifestyle decisions. This includes decisions about:

- support services
- where and with whom you live
- health care
- legal matters that do not relate to your financial or property matters

Financial matters, which relate to decisions about your financial or property affairs, including:

- paying expenses
- making investments
- selling property (including your home)
- carrying on a business

There are 2 types of powers of attorney:

- general power of attorney, which ends if you lose capacity
- enduring power of attorney, which continues if you lose capacity

Advance Care Directive and Appointment of Substitute Medical Treatment Decision Maker

What if you get hit by a bus and are still deemed medically alive but you are unable to communicate your wishes? What might you want to happen in this scenario? This is where an Enduring Power of Attorney, Advance Care Directive and/or Appointment of Substitute Medical Treatment Decision Maker come into play. If you have not appointed someone to step in and act on your behalf, the courts can order someone you may not have chosen yourself to do this.

If you have a Power of Attorney, consider the reasons you made it and whether it could be used in a scenario like the one posed above. If you don't have any of these documents, again, this is the time to create them. It can be difficult to imagine all the scenarios in which you might need someone to represent you (travelling overseas, undergoing a minor operation, concussion from a footy match - right down to stroke or the proverbial bus mishap) so take some time to ponder the *what-if's* in life and situations you might need someone to act on your behalf.

But since you've picked up this book, you're well ahead of many. You will find helpful questions throughout this book that will prompt you on what decisions are best for you. They will help you make some rational decisions if the unexpected happens, and filling out these documents will be as easy as putting on your socks for the day ahead. But before we get too carried away, let's look in greater detail at what an Advance Health Care Directive and Appointment of Substitute Medical

Treatment Decision Maker means and why we (may) need them.

MY PRIORITIES FOR END-OF-LIFE CARE

There is no point filling in these documents if you are not in touch with what is important to you at end of life. Let's dig deep and work out what is of most value to you if you are faced with a serious life-threatening situation.

Common medical end-of-life interventions for you to ponder

Australia is a country where the medical system is built to save life but not necessarily sustain quality of life. Below we will look at all the ways the system saves lives and whether these procedures are what you want when contemplating the quality of your life.

POST-DEATH DESIRES

Burial or cremation, and where? Funeral service or not? In what do you want to be buried or cremated? Who's there and who's not? How do you want to be remembered? Who gets your possessions? There are many questions here but don't worry, this is the easy part for you; it's your family that you need to consider most here.

PART II

My Death

*May your choices reflect your hopes;
not your fears.*

Nelson Mandela

STEP 1
Decide how I want to die

In this step you will work through a series of questions that will help you tease out and articulate your preferences about how you want to die. The three areas you will focus on are your values and spiritual preferences, your preferences on places you want to die, and life-sustaining treatments. After going through each of these areas, you will put together an Advance Care Directive document that draws from these desires and preferences.

This step will help you to establish what matters most to you so that you can effectively communicate it later to the ones you love, as well as any medical professionals involved.

How do I want to die?

This is a crazy question and one that we tend to tuck under the carpet and remain oblivious to, like the notion of becoming old when we are young and in our prime. But it's a question worth posing, because if you do become terminally ill or severely injured, what would you want?

Giving this some real thought and putting it down on paper will give you some sense of relief from the doom and gloom with which this question is often coloured.

So how do I answer it?

VALUES AND SPIRITUAL PREFERENCES

First, you need to consider your values and spiritual preferences. Maybe you haven't given much thought to these in the past, or maybe you have. Maybe you are heavily influenced by your family or culture, or maybe not. No matter what your values and spiritual preferences - one thing is for sure – they are likely to be unique and personal to you as an individual.

Answer the questions below to help you better articulate your thoughts and preferences.

When answering the questions, ask yourself, are your responses based on your true values and who you are spiritually? Or are your answers based on what might be expected of you by others? Let's be honest with ourselves here, okay?

Part II: My Death

What are my spiritual or religious beliefs?

_____
_____
_____
_____
_____

How do these beliefs affect my attitude about death and dying?

_____
_____
_____
_____
_____

How do these beliefs affect my attitude about terminal disease and treatment decisions?

_____
_____
_____
_____
_____

PREFERENCES ON PLACES TO DIE

There is no one 'best' place to die. The best place is wherever there is the greatest care available for that individual. Instead of thinking about 'where to die', instead consider what you desire to have around your deathbed.

Again, honestly answer the questions below to help you tease out your thoughts and preferences.

Do I want my nearest and dearest close by?

_____
_____
_____
_____
_____

Is adequate pain relief important to me?

_____
_____
_____
_____
_____

Do I want a window to look out of and do I want it open or closed?

_____
_____
_____
_____
_____

What types of lighting and sound are important?

_____
_____
_____
_____
_____

Do I want someone with me all the time or will I prefer some solitude during part of my final days?

_____
_____
_____
_____
_____

Do I have pets I want around?

_____
_____
_____
_____

Are there certain objects that are important to me, and do I want them near me?

_____
_____
_____
_____

LIFE-SUSTAINING TREATMENTS

Despite the advantages many of us have due to our medical system and its ability to keep us alive for longer, there are those whose illnesses cannot be cured or whose basic abilities to function restored. This presents a modern dilemma, requiring personal decisions about how much treatment is enough, drawing a line between therapeutic and futile treatment and deciding when to stop prolonging a life once it has ceased to become 'a life' as defined by the person living it.

Life-sustaining measures come into play when biological functions no longer maintain themselves. This may arise from illness or accident, and examples include artificial ventilation, stimulation of the heart with medication and artificial hydration and nutrition.

In Australia, life support is always initiated unless you have written documents requesting otherwise. However, Australian medical professionals are not obliged to give 'futile or non-beneficial treatment', which is decided on a case-by-case basis. This means that whether you have capacity or not, you cannot demand treatment in a situation where the medical professional believes the treatment will do more harm than good.

Advance Care Directives are designed for you to contemplate what life-sustaining treatments you definitely do **not** want if you suddenly find yourself in this scenario.

Here are some examples. Tick yes or no:

- Artificial feeding and hydration ❏ Yes ❏ No
- Cardiopulmonary resuscitation ❏ Yes ❏ No
- Assisted ventilation ❏ Yes ❏ No
- Antibiotics ❏ Yes ❏ No
- Kidney dialysis ❏ Yes ❏ No
- Blood transfusions ❏ Yes ❏ No

Your quality of life may influence these decisions, such as the ability to:

- get around by yourself
- recognise family
- communicate
- wash and feed yourself

- have control over your bladder or bowels
- remain in your home

Answer the questions below to help articulate your thoughts about these treatments.

Would I want life-sustaining treatments if there were no hope of recovery?

_____
_____
_____
_____
_____

Would my family want life-sustaining treatments for me? Have I had this conversation with them?

_____
_____
_____
_____
_____

What is my understanding of natural death, and do I want it to be allowed? Do I agree with the Euthanasia Law?

_____
_____
_____
_____
_____

Have any past experiences of healthcare shaped my attitude towards future care that I would want? These experiences can include your own or those of others.

_____
_____
_____
_____
_____

What makes my life worth living? What are the basic abilities important to me in order for me to feel as though I would want to continue living (e.g. being able to feed myself)?

_____
_____
_____
_____
_____

What is most important for me to have at my deathbed?

_____
_____
_____
_____
_____

Are there any specific life-sustaining procedures or treatments I would want or not want if I were diagnosed with a medical condition?

_____
_____
_____
_____
_____

What aspects of life are important to me? When do I believe quality of life is compromised?

_____
_____
_____
_____
_____

With respect to life-sustaining methods, how do I feel about them in the following scenarios:

Permanent unconsciousness (coma)

_____
_____
_____
_____
_____

Terminal illness

_____
_____
_____
_____
_____

Irreversible chronic condition

_____
_____
_____
_____
_____

Dementia

_____
_____
_____

What are your feelings about the following medical interventions?

Chemotherapy

_____
_____
_____

Radiation

_____
_____
_____

Mechanical breathing

_____
_____
_____

Cardiopulmonary resuscitation

_____

_____

_____

Artificial nutrition and hydration

_____

_____

_____

Surgery

_____

_____

_____

Pain relief

_____

_____

_____

Blood transfusion

_____

_____

_____

Antibiotics

_____

_____

_____

Organ transplants

_____

_____

_____

If I were suddenly faced with physical or mental limitation, how would this affect my healthcare decisions?

_____

_____

_____

_____

_____

If my condition warranted being placed in a nursing care facility, would I want that?

_____
_____
_____
_____
_____

Would I prefer palliative/hospice care over hospitalisation, with a goal to keep me comfortable in my final period of life?

_____
_____
_____
_____
_____

What are the factors that affect my decision? (e. g. pain, family members...)

_____
_____
_____
_____
_____

Do I want to participate in my healthcare decisions, or do I prefer that the professionals appointed to my care take control?

_____
_____
_____
_____

Do I always want the truth with respect to my condition and treatment options?

_____
_____
_____
_____

If my health professional has a preconceived idea of the time I have left to live, would I want to know?

_____
_____
_____
_____

On a scale of 1 – 10, 1 being low priority and 10 being of highest priority, how important are the following to me?:

Dying naturally   _____

Having family or friends close by at time of death   _____

Preserving quality of life   _____

Maximising length of life   _____

Staying true to religious beliefs and traditions   _____

Living as long as possible, without regard
to quality of life   _____

Being independent   _____

Being comfortable and pain free   _____

Dying at home in my own bed   _____

Being able to communicate with my
family and friends to the very end   _____

Avoiding expensive medical treatments   _____

Providing good memories for family and friends   _____

Partaking in medical research   _____

Retaining physical abilities   _____

Dying quickly rather than lingering   _____

Leaving money to family and friends rather
than using it to keep me alive   _____

Remaining mentally alert   _____

If my condition is terminal,
having the right to choose when I die   _____

Not compromising my family's peace of
mind due to my choices   _____

What is it that I would want if I were deemed permanently unconscious or terminally ill?

_____

_____

_____

_____

_____

Note: You may wish to talk with your family, healthcare providers and other significant people in the contemplation of these issues, remembering that this document will relieve those people of having to make these decisions on your behalf, because your wishes will already be known.

DO NOT RESUSCITATE (DNR)

If you are opposed to being resuscitated due to valid reasons regarding your condition and are of sound mind, your objection should be declared in your Advance Care Directive and promulgated to your family, support persons and medical professionals.

DNR orders are designed to come into effect after complete contemplation and a solid understanding of your condition and complications that may arise if your condition deteriorates. Therefore, they are always on a case-by-case basis.

If you complete an Advance Care Directive in good health and only have it in place for a hypothetical future accident, but your situation changes later, it may need to be reviewed. It is helpful, therefore, to regularly refresh this workbook throughout your life.

PUTTING IT ON PAPER: COMPLETE MY ADVANCE CARE DIRECTIVE

Recording your priorities and decisions in an Advance Care Directive is the cornerstone of your advance planning. This makes your decisions clear if you are unable to communicate them yourself. Let's take care of this now, and at the same time, appoint a Medical Treatment Decision Maker: someone you trust to speak on your behalf.

An **Advance Care Directive** is a legally binding document, in each Australian State and Territory, under the relevant legislation. This document creates clear obligations for health practitioners caring for people who do not have decision-making capacity.

The document is required to be signed by your GP and is to be completed when you are of sound mind. It enables you to consent to or refuse medical treatment, even if such treatment is life-saving, and will only come into effect should you lose your decision-making capacity. This document also allows you to record general statements about your values and preferences.

With the answers you have recorded above, let's put this document into effect now and at your next available opportunity take it to your GP for signing.

You can find copies of the latest Advance Care Directive forms on this website, or ask your doctor to supply one:

www.undertakinggrace.org/resources

STEP 2
Decide who will speak on my behalf

In this step you will work through the medical decisions you have already made and you will think about who in your life has the qualities needed to enact these decisions on your behalf if you no longer have the capacity to do so. At the end of this section, you will have your own 'Appointment of Medical Treatment Decision Making' document, which will designate your preferred person or people to step in if needed.

We all want someone to have our back, and when is this more important than when you are in a medical crisis and cannot speak for yourself?

MEDICAL TREATMENT DECISIONS

Your medical treatment decision maker has legal authority to make medical treatment decisions on your behalf if you do not have capacity. Only adults can appoint a Medical Treatment Decision Maker and they can appoint up to four people. Provided you have the mental capacity, you can change your Appointment of Medical Treatment Decision Maker at any time.

This is a crucial document to have if you are terminally ill or have been diagnosed with a mentally debilitating illness. Given that you are literally handing over the reins to someone else to make decisions on your behalf when you cannot, the appointment of such a person needs to be a calculated and conscious decision. What qualities do you need this person to have for you to feel assured that they will have your back and be strong enough to put things in place when you cannot?

QUALITIES OF MY DECISION MAKER

In your selection process, we encourage you to reflect on these questions:

- Will they respect my decisions?
- Are they comfortable talking about death?
- Are they assertive?
- Have they listened to and accepted my decisions so far with respect to my health choices?
- Do they live nearby?
- Do they have the emotional strength to follow through with my requests?

Early conversations matter. Remember, the person you select does not need to be your next of kin or even a family member. Who in your life do you feel comfortable giving this power to? Is there more than one person? If so, do they have the qualities needed to work as a team or in conjunction with each other?

It is helpful when appointing this person to think about how they may feel at the time. It is also helpful to understand what their values and principles are with respect to death and dying, and whether they are in alignment with your own values and principles. Once you have chosen your person, here's how you appoint them.

SPEAKING TO MY GP

Many people spend most of their adult life not having a regular GP. It wasn't until after her husband died that Claire started experiencing relentless anxiety and panic attacks. It took her a few attempts to find the right fit and when she did find someone who listened to her - really listened to her - and then went above and beyond to help her, she felt truly supported and empowered. She now recognises the importance of having a supportive doctor. How do you feel after your doctor appointments? If you feel as though you have been heard, then by all means, stick with them. If you don't feel heard, maybe it's time to shop around. The question to ask is, if the worst thing happened, *would I feel truly supported by this person?*

An Appointment of Medical Treatment Decision Maker document needs to be signed in front of and also by your doctor. Once you have decided who you want to appoint, visit your doctor to write it up together. Take note of how you feel after the doctor's appointment.

PUTTING IT ON PAPER
COMPLETE MY APPOINTMENT OF MEDICAL TREATMENT DECISION MAKER DOCUMENT

You can find copies of the latest Appointment of Medical Treatment Decision Maker documents on this website, or ask your doctor to supply one:

wwwundertakinggrace.org/resources

STEP 3
Decide who I need to tell and who family should contact

In this step you will work through what your social support currently looks like, and you will think about your current web of life. For example, who are the people and institutions that you turn to for financial, legal and personal services? At the end you will have your own 'Communication and Connection Plan', which will document everything so that you know who you need to tell about the decisions you have made (communication plan) and who your family needs to contact when death comes knocking (connection plan).

MY FAMILY

Talking with loved ones about your end-of-life care options helps establish deeper connections and greater understanding. Even some of those closest to us aren't always completely aware of our beliefs and wishes. Conversations of this nature ask us to delve deeper into what is important and can lead to new discoveries based on differing ways of thinking. Knowledge is power and gives us greater clarity for our lives and what is possible in this modern age.

If you are in a relationship that does not fit in the confines of the traditional definition of 'spouse' or 'close family member', it is also a good idea to have an addendum on your Advance Care Directive specifically stating that you want that person allowed at your deathbed. Despite progress made through marriage equality, some same-sex, gender neutral or transgender couples continue to have their preferences ignored by health professionals or family members. Decision making authority, which is automatic in heterosexual relationships, may be actively denied. This is also something to consider if you are in a de facto relationship or any relationship that is seen as controversial by other family members. Life partners of this nature have actually been refused access to one another at the deathbed and even though this seems extreme, it is always better to have written instructions submitted in a legally binding document.

Once your Advance Care Directive and Appointment of Medical Treatment Decision Maker are finalised and signed by you and your GP, make sure copies are given to:

- Your family
- Your substitute decision maker
- Your hospital and local doctor (it can reside on your MyHealth Record)
- The ambulance service
- Anyone else who you feel is appropriate

MY SOCIAL SUPPORT NETWORK

Who's in your current support network? It is good to map this out and give it to your family so they know who to contact in the event of your death.

Fill in the names below to get started:

GP _____

Senior next of kin _____

Substitute Medical Decision Maker _____

Power of Attorney _____

Solicitor _____

Accountant _____

Bank _____

Super _____

Insurer/s _____

Funeral bonds _____

Phone/Internet provider _____

Electricity/Gas provider _____

I want to stress here how important it is for people to be able to find these documents if an event arises for which they need them. Getting through authorities without them can be time-consuming and very frustrating.

Are there people I want or don't want included in any decisions with respect to my care? If so, who are they?:

_____

_____

_____

_____

_____

HEALTH, FINANCIAL & INSURANCE INSTITUTIONS

Communicating your wishes with your healthcare professional empowers you to make good healthcare decisions, and if it doesn't, consider changing to a different provider. Make sure you have the right people at your side before something unexpected happens.

Putting plans into practice means a whole lot more than filing your legal documents and letting people know where to find them. You need to make sure that your medical care professionals respect your decisions and have the ability to put them into practice for you.

Establishing an understanding with your doctor is extremely important and if they are unable to comply with your wishes, you have the right to seek the care you want from someone else.

It is also a good time now, if you have private health insurance, to check into what your provider can and cannot provide in your situation.

Also, if you are in an assisted living residency, verify that your choices are not in conflict with the policy of that institution.

After death has occurred, the bank will freeze your bank accounts unless the accounts are in joint signatories. Consider your current situation. Do you need to open an account in a name other than yours that will be designated as funds for your funeral and associated costs?

PUTTING IT ON PAPER: COMPLETE MY COMMUNICATION & CONNECTION PLAN

The single most powerful thing a person can do to improve their chance of a good death is to talk about it.

Talk to those who have the greatest impact on your care options. Talk about all the things that you have covered in this guide and get their understanding on your wishes. You can even generate a memorandum of understanding with these people to help alleviate any of your concerns.

The time is NOW to start having these discussions. It may be awkward at first but you will find continuing discussions lead to healthier, deeper, and more trusting relationships with those around you on whom you will rely in a time of need.

A great way to start these conversations is to pose a simple question. First, you must answer it yourself, though.

What do I think will happen to me when I die?

_____
_____
_____
_____
_____

Once you have spent some time pondering this question, you can start to put together your communication and connection plan. Carry out the activities below so that you can complete this plan.

Communication Plan: In the box on the following page, name everyone with whom you will need to have a discussion about your death. Put yourself in the middle of the diagram. Brainstorm all of the people surrounding you who you think could support you. Then link everyone who knows each other, and who will be able to contact each other in smaller groups.

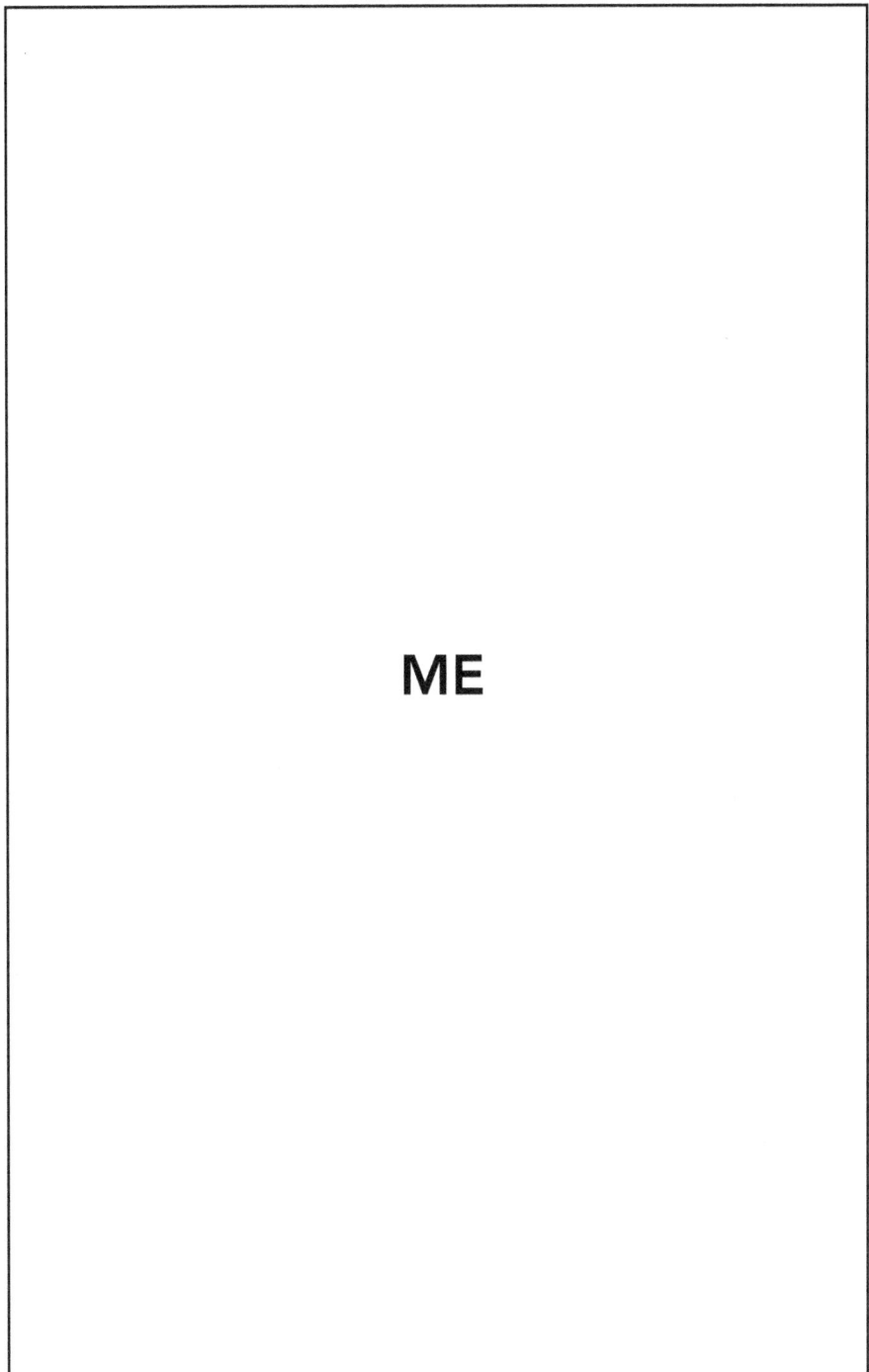

Connection Plan: In the box on the following page, name everyone who your family will need to contact. Things to consider for each person are:

Myself:

- My friendship group
- Clubs that I am a part of
- Extra-curricular activities that I am involved in
- My landlord or rental agency
- My employer or colleagues
- My hairdresser/beauty therapist/osteo/other health practitioner, etc.
- My extended family

My children

- School
- Extra-curricular activities
- Their friends

My pets

- Vet
- Any regular pet sitters or house sitters

You can find examples of communication and connection plans on this website:

www.undertakinggrace.org/resources

Part II: My Death

MY CONNECTION PLAN

STEP 4
What happens after I die?

In this step you will work through your post-death choices and think about what you wish to leave for your loved ones. At the end, you will have answered all of the questions and have all the key ingredients to create your own 'Will, Funeral Plan & Letters of Love'. Some of the questions might be challenging, but not as challenging as if you leave them for someone else (whom you may not even choose) to answer. Feel confident in your choices and relieved that you are doing this now.

CHOICES FOR MY BODY

We have gone through some nitty gritty stuff already so if you haven't yet, take a moment, get a cup of tea or a glass of wine and take a break, giving yourself a pat on the back for making it this far!

Whilst you enter this next contemplation, concentrate on the family members around you who are likely to be living through your death. Think about how, if you write down your ideals now, it will lessen the pressure on them at a time of sorrow and vulnerability.

Do I want to be buried or cremated?

_____

_____

_____

_____

_____

If I prefer burial, where?

_____

_____

_____

_____

_____

If I prefer cremation, what do I want done with my ashes?

_____
_____
_____
_____
_____

Have you considered paying for your funeral or cremation in advance? Many funeral directors offer a pre-paid service, for example the Australian company *Bare* has a comprehensive website showing how cost effective and simple a pre-paid cremation service can be to organise.

_____
_____
_____
_____
_____

More information can be found on www.bare.com.au

Generally, on your passing there will be a ceremony organised for family and friends to come together in mourning. Are there any special requests you have with respect to such a ceremony? For example:

Is there any particular music I would like played?

_____
_____
_____
_____
_____

Is there a specific place I would like the ceremony to be held?

_____
_____
_____
_____
_____

Any particular quotes or passages that I would like included in the ceremony?

_____
_____
_____
_____
_____

What about photos? Do I have a favourite photo of myself or with anyone else that I want included?

_____
_____
_____
_____
_____

Would I like to be buried or cremated with anything special?

_____
_____
_____
_____
_____

Any other special requests?

_____
_____
_____
_____
_____

DEATH NOTICES

Death notices are printed at the time of someone's death to spread the message far and wide to anyone who may not be in direct communication with you or your family. It is a good idea to document now which newspapers you'd like your family to run the notice in, and to let them know your thoughts about this.

_____

_____

_____

_____

_____

PEOPLE TO TELL

It is helpful to create lists now of people who will need to be told (or not told!) of your death. Consider the social networks you've made throughout your lifetime. Doing this can be a beautifully reflective time. And once again, if they are given a clear set of instructions and the knowledge of where and how to contact people, it will lessen the pressure on your family.

_____

_____

_____

_____

PEOPLE, PETS AND POSSESSIONS

You already have a Will in place and this should designate guardianship of children and how you would like your assets to be disbursed. However, in most Wills, concentration is generally on the assets of significant value, i.e. land, property, shares, etc.

It's time now to contemplate the important *people* in your life and personal items of significance that are not included in your Will. You might have some jewellery, a painting, or a favourite chair that would mean a great deal to special friend.

Is there anything you have that you wish to share with the wider community that you may not have thought about before?

Any special items I have and who I want them to go to.

_____

_____

_____

_____

_____

_____

_____

_____

_____

_____

What pets do I have and where would I like them to go upon my passing?

_____
_____
_____
_____
_____

Anything further?

_____
_____
_____
_____
_____

LOVE LETTERS

We humans are such transient souls, we never know how long we are destined to live. Thinking about our mortality creates the space to think about what we truly wish to share with our beloveds. We are not always given the time and space to speak words of love to the people to whom we give our love. Writing love letters can be a beautiful and reflective process and an absolute gift to the person on the receiving end.

Consider writing some love letters.

PUTTING IT ON PAPER
COMPLETE YOUR WILL, FUNERAL PLAN & LETTERS OF LOVE

You can find links to help you create your will, funeral plan & letters of love on the website:

www.undertakinggrace.org/resources

REVISIT, REFLECT & REVIEW
HANDY TIPS FOR KEEPING IT CURRENT

Contemplating your death whilst you are still alive may feel uncomfortable and you might feel that it's not the time to think about things of this nature. However, regardless of your stage of life or health, at the very least ponder this eventuality. Arming yourself with the knowledge of your own contemplations is the best weapon you can have when death comes knocking, because it *will* come.

Bhutan is reportedly the happiest place on earth. Why? Because they spend numerous moments every day contemplating their own mortality.

Using this workbook continuously in your life and updating it regularly when your circumstances change will lead you to feeling more empowered about life and about death.

Every now and then you should reflect on the process from Steps 1 to 4.

You have the authority to change your Advance Care Directive at any time. One thing we're all guaranteed in life is change, and through your future experiences, your ideas and beliefs may change. You are able to revoke both of your documents and submit more relevant versions.

Check to make sure that your designated representative is still the person you wish to speak for you and that their circumstances have not changed.

When travelling far from home or for long periods of time, consider taking a copy with you. Although the Advance Care Directives differ on a state-by-state basis, most states will recognise a valid Advance Care Directive, although there may be some limitations and/or additional requirements. Similarly, an appointment of Substitute Medical Treatment Decision Maker will usually apply, but be mindful of differing legislations from state to state.

If you are moving interstate or planning to be outside of your state for an extended period of time, it is best to contact the Office of Public Advocate in the intended State or Territory to find out more information.

PART III

My life

May your dreams be larger than mountains and may you have the courage to scale their summits.

Harley King

PEACE

Reflect on your life and the people who shaped it, moments in time that were filled with immense joy or sorrow. Issues that arose throughout your relationships and how you dealt with them…

Is there anything I have left unsaid?

_____

_____

_____

_____

_____

_____

_____

_____

_____

_____

_____

_____

_____

_____

_____

_____

_____

_____

How would I approach life if I knew the end date was soon?

_____
_____
_____
_____
_____
_____
_____
_____

Are there experiences that I crave, and have not yet prioritised?

_____
_____
_____
_____
_____
_____
_____
_____

How are my current relationships and how can I improve them?

___

WHAT IS MY LEGACY?

What is the legacy that I would like to leave? How do I want to be remembered?

___

LIFE REVIEW

There is an old African proverb that says 'When an elder dies, a whole library burns down'. Elder wisdom comes not from the accumulation of knowledge, but from reflecting on life. Instead of living in a state of unworthiness and regret, we can grieve and forgive the past, find redemption in our story and recognise how it fits into our ancestral mythos. This work becomes our gift to the future. Consider undertaking a Life Review. For further information, contact info@undertakinggrace.com

CHECKLIST OF NECESSARY ITEMS

- ❏ A Last Will and Testament
- ❏ An Enduring Power of Attorney
- ❏ An Advance Care Directive or Medical Power of Attorney
- ❏ Appointment of a Substitute Decision Maker
- ❏ A pre-paid funeral plan

Where are these documents located?

_____

_____

Who is the designated Executor of my Will?

_____

_____

Do I understand that the Executor has the legal right to decide what happens to my body after I die?

☐ Yes   ☐ No

Have I made my wishes clear to them?

_____

_____

Do I have a death benefit in my superannuation fund or life insurance policy?

_____

_____

If yes, where and with whom is it located?

_____

_____

Do I wish to be considered for organ donation?

_____

_____

If yes, have I registered on the donatelife.gov.au website?
_____
_____

Do I have a joint bank account?
_____
_____

Do I have an account set up (not in my name) for emergencies?
_____
_____

If so, where?
_____
_____

What is the passcode on my phone/laptop?
_____
_____

What is/are the password/s on my email accounts?
_____
_____

Who is my accountant?
_____
_____

Who is my lawyer?
_____
_____

What money is direct debited from my accounts?
_____
_____
_____
_____

On what date of the month are these funds drawn?
_____
_____
_____
_____

For my business, what accounting system is in place?

_____

_____

What is the password?

_____

_____

Is my bookkeeping kept up to date weekly, monthly or quarterly?

_____

_____

Is there a current record of money owed and money owing?

_____

_____

Part III: My Life

I _____ am creating this document so that my family, caregivers, healthcare professionals, support workers and other loved ones will be aware of and honour my wishes with respect to my death.

_____

Signature

_____

Date

_____   _____

Witness Name   Witness Signture

_____

Witness Address and Phone Contact

_____

Witness Date

(Note: Please sign and date each page of this book and any attached documentation)

We live in such a death-phobic society here in Australia but it doesn't need to be that way. Our lives are just as mysterious as our death, we never truly know what's around the corner. We think that if we can blend the idea of life and death together and not see them as such polar opposites, we will have a better time at navigating them both.

This book was created through both heart wrenching and dream fulfilling times and we appreciate your time with it. We hope that it can help you piece together what's important and that it helps you to lead a more compassionate and fulfilling life.

Claire & Rose

www.ingramcontent.com/pod-product-compliance
Lightning Source LLC
Chambersburg PA
CBHW020330010526
44107CB00054B/2053